Dedicated with much love

to my wonderful family

Stephen,
Matt and Naori,
Jenny and Russell

for always being there

CONTENTS

WHAT'S IT ALL ABOUT?

Professionalism is a choice, an opportunity for you to think, behave and act in a way which will make you stand out from the crowd.

Professionalism is not just for those who work in the traditional professions. It is for you and me and all of our colleagues and friends, whether we are students, doctors or architects, work in a factory, a coffee shop, an office or anywhere else that we come in contact with others. It is for everyone, at all stages of our careers and at all levels of every organisation.

This book offers you an insight into the ways that professionals approach their world and offers some very practical advice, intended to help you demonstrate your own professionalism 24/7.

Make a decision to adopt an attitude and a skill set which will ensure that you always look, sound and act in ways which inspire trust and confidence in those around you.

Definitions of professionalism are hard to come by and some say that those who exude professionalism have a 'certain something' – hard to put your finger on but you know it when you see it. It is about something in a person's manner, their abilities, the way they speak, the way they dress, their obvious standards, all of which add up to a powerful presence and all of which you recognise as professional.

That's not overly helpful is it? What we do know is that it is about the total package, not just adopting one or two superficial signs which you hope that people will interpret as professionalism – a snappy suit or a smart business card. This book will help you to identify all of the elements which contribute to the final goal and show you that it is attainable for everyone.

 'Professionalism is knowing how to do it, when to do it and actually doing it'
Frank Tyger

Professionalism applies to all of us, all the time, not just in the workplace but in our personal lives as well. It's about everything we are and everything we do. So this book applies to individuals and also to the organisations where we work. Encourage your colleagues to read it and ask your employers to adopt its message for the entire workforce.

If you know that just getting by isn't enough and that there must be something missing – professionalism is the answer. It will change the way you look at the world and will have a remarkable effect on how the world treats you in return.

Read this, keep it in your pocket, dip in and out to remind yourself of its contents every so often and you will be amazed at the results.

Susie Kay
London
January 2010

CHOOSE EXCELLENCE

CHOOSE EXCELLENCE

We are all used to the idea that society applauds excellence in a variety of ways. We see award ceremonies for the 'best of' everything, from films to books, from holiday companies to advertisements; we hear about prestigious prizes for inventive or ground-breaking ideas; we understand that reaching the top of your profession can attract a larger salary.

Excellence is also the root of professionalism. It is about putting in maximum effort, not just to get something done but to achieve the best possible result and to do it with passion!

An individual's choice not to accept second rate or second best for themselves or those around them means not just looking at the big ideas and issues but paying attention to the little things too. They all make a difference. We can't deny that the big issues, such as maintaining standards and always behaving ethically, are incredibly important but the smaller signs of excellence, apparent in the way we treat other people and in the way we behave each day, are just as important.

Striving for the professionalism ideal is not enough by itself. That ideal needs to translate our thoughts and attitudes into actions, words into deeds, to make a difference. So we need to look at the elements which will help you to support your choice - your attitude, your behaviour and your character – to enhance your professionalism and provide you with the **ABC for success**.

MAKING A START

All great endeavours need a jumping off point. All projects need a start-up meeting. All great ideas have a key moment of inspiration. All great recipes need an ingredient list! So in your journey towards professionalism you also need to make a start.

Make a note today in your diary, or on your wall, as a visible reminder that TODAY is the start of your journey toward professionalism

That starting point is your decision to choose excellence. This is your first and most important choice and it will colour everything you do from this point forwards. There is a very old saying 'if something is worth doing, then it is worth doing well'. Let's take it a step further and say that it is worth striving for and delivering excellence in everything you do.

With excellence as your eventual goal, and the pursuit of excellence as the companion on your journey, you will find that you will:

- Enhance your own performance
- Maintain the quality and accuracy of everything you do
- Bring enthusiasm and passion to all that you do
- Develop a 'can-do' response to tasks and challenges
- Take ownership of problems and be a creative problem solver
- Use your initiative to act on opportunities whenever possible
- Seek and not fear responsibility
- Look for anything which can be improved
- Not hesitate in suggesting and introducing improvements
- Go the extra mile, the extra effort that makes a difference to the outcome
- Respect and appreciate the contribution of others
- Encourage others to do more or better
- Continue your learning in all areas

EXCELLENCE ALL THE TIME!

You will be aiming for excellence at all times, even when you don't feel like it. When you have a bad head cold, or the train was late, or your car broke down, you will need to get beyond all of that in order to continue to meet your own high standards as well as the expectations of others.

    Don't deviate from your own high expectations and standards!

We are all affected by difficulties at some times in our lives and it would be a rare day which was completely trouble or hassle-free. The trick, however, is not to transfer that trouble to others around you. Remember that your agenda is not theirs, neither should your problems be an issue for them. Your day-to-day persona and your dealings with people should be consistent, as far as possible, so that they know what to expect in their interactions with you.

From your perspective, focussing entirely on the work or task in hand may just help to get your day back in focus and get you back on an even keel!

    Your main focus is not inside yourself but outside, concentrating on your tasks and on other people

YOU AND THE REST OF THE WORLD

Although the elements in this book are designed to help you develop your own professionalism, the real story starts to emerge when you realise that the changes in you are mainly about changes in the value you place on others, as well as in how you apply your own abilities.

Your determination to be the best you can possibly be should mean that others around you will expect excellence from you and, in this way, your reputation for professionalism and as a trustworthy individual will grow and support you in all you do.

As a professional, you will continually work to achieve and implement high standards, working to your own internal moral and ethical codes as well as to any specific requirements from your chosen profession. You will also work to the highest quality standards, making these demands on yourself without others having to remind you of them.

A for ATTITUDE

A for ATTITUDE

A for ATTITUDE

It is never too early or too late to realise that professionalism applies to all of us, all of the time, not just in the workplace but in your personal life as well. Being the sort of person who is known to be trustworthy, honourable, honest and reliable brings its own rewards.

Professionalism is not linked to your job title or how many qualifications you have achieved. It is about the type of person you choose to be and about the effort and integrity with which you tackle whatever comes your way.

These attributes are the difference between professionalism and just doing your job. They bring the self-belief to tackle the unknown with confidence and to deliver every time.

"We all underestimate what we can achieve…"
Tim Smit, creator of The Eden Project. Currently a social innovator, previously an archaeologist and music producer

If you could grow professionalism in a test tube or create it from a recipe book then you would find a long list of ingredients needed to make your final product. There are some indispensable components and some which may not be quite so obvious. Let's look at them one by one.

TRUSTWORTHY

Above all else, to be described as worthy of someone's trust is the bedrock on which we build all the other attributes which contribute to the make-up of true professionalism.

To be trustworthy means that you can be trusted, without hesitation, with people, tasks, resources, confidences, secrets or responsibility. Others will be secure in the knowledge that, whatever has been asked of you, it will be carried out efficiently, effectively, and conscientiously. It is taken for granted that you will meet deadlines and produce work of superior quality and fully meet your commitments.

 You are always as good as your word and can be relied on without hesitation

We all have a responsibility to be trustworthy, not just to ourselves but to each other as well. As a word of caution, however, trust can be easily lost and is almost impossible to re-establish once it is gone. Recent public events, such as those in the banking industry and in the Houses of Parliament, have shown just how bad things can get if levels of trust between large chunks of the population disintegrate.

Never assume that your needs are more important than others or assume that people will understand or forgive your motivations. Many of the MPs implicated in the recent expenses controversy sought to explain their misdemeanours by stating that they were acting within the rules or had been given permission for the claims they made. Neither of these excuses could explain how they did not see that their actions would be perceived as clearly wrong from any external viewpoint. The result was a further perception that these individuals felt that they were above the law and could no longer, therefore, be trusted with the governing process.

It is as well to remember that we all judge others by our own standards.

 People are paying attention. Be an ambassador not an embarrassment

PASSIONATE

You are passionate about what you do and you are not afraid to show people that you enjoy doing it. Passion turns the ordinary into the extraordinary and makes it worth getting up in the morning.

Letting others see your passion for the subject or task in hand can make a difference in whether or not your particular project is implemented or it may be sufficient to motivate others to work with you to achieve something new.

It may also be the only thing that gets you through the hard times, when no one else believes as you do or the day-to-day detail starts to nibble away at your enthusiasm.

You always stand up for yourself and your ideals. If you believe in something, you say so. If you have an opinion, you share it. There are plenty of others who may want to come along for the ride.

 Be happy in what you do – it's contagious!

RELIABLE

We all need to know that we can depend on others around us, whether it is for completing a project on time, for help with our wedding arrangements or organising the school run rota. You must be willing to be someone on whom others can depend. It takes effort and constant attention but, over time, becomes second nature.

If you are reliable you will:

- Live up to your commitments and meet your obligations

- Keep your word and do what you say you will

- Take your job, or the task in hand, seriously

- Be an effective part of any team

- Look for what is needed or wanted and deliver it

- Go the extra mile to ensure completion

- Add value to everything that you do

- Be where you are supposed to be

You will also:

- Get the basics right

- Be a problem solver

- Radiate an air of confidence and credibility

- Be diligent and dedicated to the task in hand

HOW NOT TO DO IT!

Think about how often people let you down. It may not be intentional but the disappointment or annoyance is very real. They don't call to set up the lunch they offered; they don't send that document you are waiting for; they don't remember your birthday; the list is endless. Do not be someone who is known for those sorts of omissions.

You definitely do not want to be known as someone who cannot make a commitment. A recent story illustrates this quite clearly. A business consultant was asked to keep a date free in the diary for a particular piece of work and waited some time for confirmation and details. When she was finally able to reach her contact she was told that he had received a more entertaining offer for that date and was doing something else. This is probably not the most effective way to maintain a business relationship. If you make a commitment then stick to it, even if you do get a better offer.

It doesn't matter how good your memory normally is, we all suffer from information overload at some time so make notes – lots of them – electronically or on paper, whatever works for you. Use any tool which will help you to avoid memory failures, double-booking or outright mistakes.

 Don't rely on your memory alone – information overload can have worrying results! Make notes and check them regularly.

Be someone who can be relied on to do what is asked or required, on time and with good grace. Don't just get by, produce more than is expected. If someone likes you, your efficiency and the way you do business (or provide a service) then they will RE-MEMBER being treated well and come back for more.

 We can all be reliable and thoughtful of the needs of others – don't become known as someone who never delivers

DETERMINED

If you always look at short term requirements you will only cure immediate issues. You should also think in the medium and long term so that you remain proactive not merely reactive to current situations.

You will have an overview, always seeing the bigger picture, which offers clarity and an ability to plan ahead.

You will maintain your overall perspective and avoid being sidetracked. Your expectations are focused in real time and are not subject to the whims of others.

 Avoid being sidetracked. It will knock you off course

You have a positive outlook and look forward to each day's challenges.

If others ask more of you than you can offer at that moment, be clear about how and when you will be able to assist them or come back to the discussion they need to have with you. Very few things are so urgent that they cannot wait for an hour or two or until you have finished your current task.

 If you have an assignment which must be complete by the end of the day, be polite but firm with all those who call you or knock on your door and want to talk about a different piece of work or just have a chat

You will be able to distinguish those issues which need your immediate attention but it has to be your decision to allow it to intrude, not someone else's.

HELPFUL

In order to make a meaningful contribution, professionals seek to understand the bigger picture, not just their own role or task but how it fits with everyone and everything else.

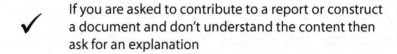 If you are asked to contribute to a report or construct a document and don't understand the content then ask for an explanation

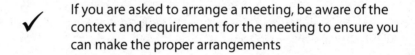 If you are asked to arrange a meeting, be aware of the context and requirement for the meeting to ensure you can make the proper arrangements

To adopt a professional approach and to think, behave and act as a professional then your intentions will be reflected in deeds or actions. Everything you do will be designed to be of assistance to others, perhaps helping them to achieve their own goals or working with them to achieve an employer's or society's requirements.

To be helpful then you are also willing to do what is asked of you, to make changes when necessary or to adapt to current circumstances – even if it was not on your own agenda for the day. That is not to say that you must abandon your own needs every time but it does mean that you will need to find an appropriate response to a request for assistance!

You look for ways to make improvements in what you are currently doing or in something you are planning, to enhance effectiveness and efficiency, taking a mental step back from what is familiar, to see if you can find any alternatives. Ask others for their opinion, start a discussion, collect suggestions.

 Worth remembering is the famous 'bigger picture' story of the janitor who was mopping the floor in an aircraft hangar at NASA when a visiting dignitary arrived. When asked what he was doing, his response was *'I'm helping to put a man on the moon'.* Man with a purpose!

ADAPTABLE

Closed minds achieve little and often find themselves stuck in a rut and unable to find a way out so be open to new ideas.

Look for opportunities to be involved with people you haven't worked with before, perhaps in areas which may be new to you or which offer a chance to work at a more senior level than usual.

Consider tackling something which you have gone out of your way to avoid in the past just so that you can say that you have actually tried!

Try not to refuse outright if asked to step out of your comfort zone but consider all the angles before making a decision.

Identify any problems which may be hampering you or your colleagues and be part of the solution.

Start each day by setting out the detail for your personal to-do list.

Making your choices and prioritising means that you know what will fit into your day. It will also mean that you can distinguish between what is important and what would be nice to have the time to do.

Be flexible and politely take the unexpected or intrusions in your stride but only accept what you can find time for by reorganising what is already there. You cannot add to your list without amending it or deferring tasks as you will eventually run the risk of non-delivery. If you really cannot fit it in don't just offer 'I don't have time' as your explanation. Explain when you will be able to do it and why it will be slightly delayed.

Careful planning avoids, as far as possible, urgent matters cropping up but it will never prevent a crisis from occurring. Deal with these in a calm, efficient way.

 Be available, help when and where you can,
ensure your door is open (within reason)

APPROACHABLE

A key expression of your professionalism will be your relationships with other people. Balance the requirements of your obligations, which you have earned because of your level of knowledge and skills, with how you use that knowledge to work with others.

Do not build barriers between yourself and others or keep them at a distance. You realise that understanding people, and the relationships between them, is the glue that binds you to other people and which holds teams together.

A smile costs nothing, it is believed to use fewer muscles than a frown, and is a wonderful way to show that you are willing to have a conversation or build an ongoing relationship. In fact, in a 2002 study in Sweden, researchers confirmed that people respond in kind to the facial expressions they meet, instinctively responding smile to smile or frown to frown, and finding it very difficult to comply when asked to do the opposite – responding to a frown with a smile.

 Good humour and good manners are essential

Co-operating and getting along with other people is essential. Be a useful, supportive, contributing team member.

Offer leadership whenever it is appropriate and ensure that you have the skills and competence to back it up. Be a good role model to those watching you for leadership and look for opportunities to offer yourself in a mentoring role. You will have the ability to nurture someone less experienced whilst having expectations that others will also step up to the mark.

You always pay attention and listen carefully, to ensure your understanding is clear, not just superficial. You are always interested and concentrate on one person at a time, as each is worthy of your full attention. This makes others feel that both they, as individuals, and their contributions are important to you and the task in hand. We have probably all experienced the discomfort of talking to someone at a party or a conference and seeing them glance around or watch the door. You just know they are not concentrating on you.

Listening is a powerful tool and it is hard work. Take the time to practice.

RESPECTFUL

Having and showing respect for others is a very powerful component of professionalism. Treating others as you would wish them to treat you is an empowering lesson to learn. How you treat others and your actions will have an effect on everything you are able to achieve.

Most parents will attempt to show or teach their children the right and wrong way to do things and how to interact with people. In this way children learn to identify the limits of acceptable behaviour and recognise that stepping outside those limits might have repercussions. We continue that learning process as adults and add to our understanding of what is appropriate behaviour in particular situations.

Respect is an interesting and complex idea which has two sides. Most would agree that respect should be earned but also that we should show respect for rules and for those in authority, due to their rank or position. However, if the rules or the actions of individuals run contrary to the ethical code or standards by which a professional lives then this creates a dilemma and will need to be addressed.

Remember – nobody is so important that they can treat others as insignificant. Everyone should have a voice. Respect your colleagues and the contribution they can make. Inspire others and encourage them to contribute and participate.

Finally, earn respect for your professionalism from others and demonstrate that you respect yourself. This does not mean getting wrapped up in your own importance. Everyone can be replaced and it is better to train and empower others to take over from you when your task is finished. Leave a legacy by passing on your knowledge and skills.

At some point in your life someone is likely to go out of their way to give you a helping hand. Take every opportunity to pass that on or pay it forward. Help others in their career and personal lives. This will inevitably enhance your reputation as a 'safe pair of hands' and someone who will offer good advice.

 Respect is earned – it is not an entitlement

B for BEHAVIOUR

B for BEHAVIOUR

Behaviour, conduct, actions, call it what you will, the second component of your ABC for Success is the part of you that you share with the rest of the world.

The way you behave, both in private and in public, has an effect on you and on those around you.

Even if you were to live a solitary, hermit-like existence in some remote out-of-the-way place, these days you would probably still make contact with a number of other people, if only by the grace of electronic communication. For most of us the day is filled with countless interactions, from the moment we wake up in the morning – the friends and family we live with, the staff in the shop where we buy our newspaper or our coffee, our fellow commuters, work colleagues, fellow students, phone calls, emails, meetings, conferences, the staff in restaurants we visit, social events, and on and on...

In each of these circumstances and on every occasion, remember that the way people experience their interactions with you makes a lasting impression. Make sure it is all positive!

  People will forget what you said
People will forget what you did
But people will never forget how you made them feel

ETHICS, MORALS AND STANDARDS

This is a fundamental issue and one which is non-negotiable. Your behaviour is always driven by ethical considerations.

Professionalism requires that you always work to extremely high standards, both of morals and of quality, set by yourself and possibly also externally if you belong to one of the many professional bodies and membership associations which will provide codes of conduct or practice for your particular profession or skillset.

These standards by which we live and work define us – the personal and work ethics in which we believe and which colour our decision making in every sphere of activity with which we are involved.

 'Doing the right thing may not always be the
easiest path but it keeps you looking forward
not over your shoulder'

You know and do what is necessary in every situation, even if you don't feel like it. You never do what is not right and, should you be asked to do so, your internal codes prevent you from agreeing. This can potentially bring you into conflict with others around you, perhaps if asked to do something by a superior or a friend with which you are not comfortable. Although this may be challenging to deal with on a personal level, the result is never in doubt.

Professionals do not allow any cracks to appear in their ethical make up. It is possible to maintain and demonstrate your passion and enthusiasm but still be able to stand up for yourself and your ideals.

 The definition of ideology:
a set of ideas with a strong social influence

Professionalism is an ideology. Its application to all areas of work, to all sectors of the economy and to all group interactions should have a major influence for the good because ethical behaviour can also be contagious.

MANNERS MATTER

Your professionalism means that you are unfailingly polite and courteous at all times. Saying please and thank you for even the smallest of things is empowering for you and the recipient.

You let people see that you have a sense of humour. It draws people to you and is a valuable tool in building relationships. Good moods can be infectious and we know that having fun is critical for our wellbeing. Your professional 'radar' will tell you if there are tasks to finish before you allow yourself to indulge in some downtime.

 Smile – it's good for you and for those around you

The personal touch can also bring dividends. Always offering the added extras, remembering birthdays, sending thank you notes, become an integral part of the way you conduct yourself. It may be better to make a phone call rather than sending an email, especially if the situation is a little difficult. Sending a personal note will give a different emphasis to your communication than sending an email.

Spare a thought for the young man who lost his job because he fell out of favour with his boss. During a team paintball event he managed to hit the boss at close range, causing a fair amount of pain. His error was not in the damage he inflicted but in choosing to wait till the next day to apologise and then doing it by email. An immediate apology and a personal visit to follow it up would have shown his sincerity in the circumstances and may have been effective in preventing his subsequent slide from grace!

Good manners, acts of kindness and thoughtfulness cost nothing but your effort. The difference they make to your interactions with others, however, is remarkable and worth noting as you go about your daily routines.

 Have you noticed how someone serving you coffee with a smile can start your day off just right?

Prepare well and arrive on time for discussions or meetings – this is also basic good manners. Noting everyone's name as they introduce themselves demonstrates that you care who they are, what they are doing there and will assist you to remember them next time you meet!

Arriving on time for meetings also means being ready to begin work at the allotted start time. Try not to be the person who delays the start of the meeting while you get a cup of coffee or look for your pen.

Help anyone who asks but be aware that not everyone will find it easy to ask for help or what they actually want, even if they are really in need. Being intuitive or sensing that someone is in need is a really useful talent which will allow you to look for ways in which to be helpful to those who can't or don't ask. There are likely to be some clues or hints which could help you in understanding the nature of what is needed. Check the body language and try to read between the lines – even with the spoken word! If you think that this is not an area you are comfortable with then there are lots of good reference guides which will show you the basics – which is all you really need, you don't need to be an expert to boost your abilities enough to make a difference.

 'As you grow older you will discover that you have two hands, one for helping yourself and one for helping others'
  - *Audrey Hepburn*

ALWAYS PRESENT A PROFESSIONAL IMAGE

Professionals will normally take quite a lot of care when preparing for a job interview, making sure that you have done some research and know a little something about the organisation you are attempting to join. You have checked over your CV, have thought about the questions they might ask and prepared your answers. That's not the end of the story though, is it? You will also put some thought into what to wear, whether to take a document case and how much travelling time is needed. Turning up looking unkempt or hot and bothered is not a great idea.

Have you ever asked yourself why you do all this preparation? The answer is simple. You want to make a good impression and, in reality, you only have a very few seconds when meeting someone for the first time to fix that picture in their mind. We are meeting new people and walking into new situations all the time so we need to create the right impression every time.

 You never get a second chance to make a first impression

We know it is important to behave appropriately, whatever the situation, so we don't let our standards slip. As our professionalism grows, having a touch of grace, elegance and timing about what we do and how we present ourselves will become second nature.

Just occasionally there will be situations where your usual style could be out of step with the norm for a particular place or organisation. If you suspect this may be the case, a little forward planning and research can ensure that you don't turn up in a suit when no-one in the company wears one. However, you won't want to wear a tatty pair of jeans either so always arrive looking like you have made an effort.

PROFESSIONAL MATURITY

Professional maturity will give you taste and timing, knowing what is appropriate and how to act in any situation.

As professionals you continue to grow both emotionally and professionally over time but, in general, your approach will be consistent with both your maturity and your experience.

There may be occasions when your behaviour needs to be amended just a little to fit a particular set of circumstances. This does not mean that the change is permanent or that it would happen at all if the changes required were entirely in opposition to your normal personality.

 If a respected male colleague behaves inappropriately to female colleagues after drinking too much at a conference dinner, he should not be surprised when he loses that respect as a consequence.

There is a time and place for everything and understanding how particular behaviours fit particular circumstances is a critical test of your maturity. A sense of humour is an effective tool in the workplace, especially as a way of diffusing potentially difficult or embarrassing moments.

However, humour may not be appropriate in a situation which calls for decisive or strong leadership. Bringing people from different backgrounds together to work on a group project may require some strong discipline or a light touch. Every case will be different and there is no magic formula – except your skill in dealing with it.

PERFORMANCE

Professionalism means encouraging high expectations. As a result, you are expected to produce results where talking, thinking and planning are converted into actions and delivery.

Good organisation and time management are essential tools. At the same time it would be hard to under-estimate the importance of planning and preparation. Setting priorities for the day, the week, the month ahead and planning in the short, medium and long term will be effective for any activity and allow you to organise resources to ensure that you meet those priorities.

Each of us has preferred ways of working and these patterns are usually set early, becoming more effective as we continue to refine them.

The enhancements and opportunities that technology now offers are a boon but do not be intimidated by that technology if you prefer paper or other traditional methods. It is your choice but be sure to stay up to date to prevent missing out on anything which might prove to be useful.

Being organised means many things to different individuals but may include:

- Knowing where you are supposed to be at all times and arriving on time
- Knowing what your schedule requires for the coming months
- Ensuring that you have your own equipment or supplies for any situation
- If you are responsible for a meeting, arriving early to ensure everything is ready
- Working in an area which is kept clear and orderly
- Ensuring that you know where to find documentation
- Keeping contact details up to date and available
- Providing clear explanations

Essential to any commitment you make is the requirement to finish the task. Know when that is likely to happen and if, by chance, delays are going to occur, be able to say when the expected time or date for completion will be. If it is necessary or helpful then set up a review or follow-up process and ensure that it is also completed by the due date.

Being persistent, remaining focused and clear headed as well as being level headed and optimistic will also help in achieving deadlines and commitments.

A professional will never say that he has not yet been told how to do something, he will go and find the answer for himself – he is pro-active not passive. Try not to emulate the behaviour of the civil servant who had been in post for just over six months. At a department training session each employee was asked how they were getting on and what they had learned since they had joined. The individual in question replied that he had not yet had his induction so he hadn't been able to learn anything yet, thereby demonstrating that he was not just lazy but also uninterested and without the ability to be self reliant. What results would you expect from his next appraisal session?

BE RESPONSIVE

Responsiveness is one of the golden rules. We all know how aggravating it is not to receive a promised or expected response and that applies to both important and less serious matters. Perhaps you have sent in a job application and not received an acknowledgement that it has been received or when to expect a result. Perhaps you have asked a friend if they could give you a lift into college next week but they don't get back to you to make arrangements.

At the end of any conversation, meeting or transaction of any kind, go over your notes or think about what has been discussed and ensure that you know what actions are expected, by whom and by when. If you are unclear then check with someone else who was present to make sure your understanding is correct.

Set the expectations about how and when you will respond. If for any reason it later becomes clear that targets are going to be missed then an immediate message is needed. In positive language, apologise for the delay, re-set the expectations and be sure that your recipient is clear about the new arrangements.

The need to be responsive can also be much more immediate. Giving someone your full attention, being 'present' in the moment, so that you really hear what they are saying, both verbally and by other signals, means that you cannot be distracted by other claims on your attention.

SELF CONTROL

Behave with dignity in all situations. That is not to say that you have to be serious all the time but know that your self-discipline is an important element of your overall professional demeanour. Self-control and maturity can be found in any age group and are not just the domain of the more experienced parts of the population. Let your inner voice guide you.

On the down side, if you exhibit immature or ill-considered behaviour it can have serious or unforeseen consequences for you as an individual and your future opportunities. There have been several recent examples of job applicants whose 'out-of-hours' activities have found their way onto Facebook and convinced potential future employers to offer the job elsewhere.

One of the most difficult lessons we all learn is that if you make a mistake then there is bound to be an audience!

You should therefore avoid:

- Using offensive language
- Making derogatory remarks
- Indulging in gossip
- Making unpleasant jokes at a colleague's expense. Think how it would feel to be on the receiving end and think twice before hurting someone's feelings in this way

Deal with difficult situations rationally and calmly. Maintain your cool and your own professionalism. Don't react to unprofessional behaviour in other people in a similar vein – whatever the provocation.

COMMUNICATION

In theory it is not difficult to communicate. It's all around us so we know what we are doing, don't we? Well, possibly not all the time. The enormous range of formats by which we can now communicate presents the challenge of matching the most appropriate mode of communication to a particular task or individual or set of circumstances. It can be a minefield where minor mistakes can lead to major errors and potential catastrophes – remember the paintball incident?

'The single biggest problem in communication is the illusion that it has taken place'
- *George Bernard Shaw*

The first requirement for being a good communicator is to realise that this is a two way process. We must both receive and transmit – listen and talk. Think about using the 80:20 ratio for the optimum proportions of listening to talking.

As a result of good communications habits your default setting will be in receive mode – making you open to hearing or finding out information that might not otherwise come your way. Asking the right questions is another route to understanding as the answers should then precisely fit the gaps in your existing knowledge.

You also want your communications to have the right impact, whatever the format. It is worth taking some time to understand what good practice for each of the formats means. Whether it is using email, blogging, writing newsletters or making phone calls, the technology or software is a blank canvas so it is dependent on the sender to make the message absolutely clear and to give it a 'voice', thereby conveying meaning and personality.

Remember to pause and re-read your emails before you press the 'send' button to avoid spelling or 'mood' errors

It is also worth remembering that all technologies are tools which will supplement but not always replace face-to-face as the most effective form of communication whenever possible. The way you speak and hold a conversation will tell people a lot more than is immediately obvious. It will also give them clues about where you come from, your education and your attitude toward the subject you are discussing, whether that is about work or something more personal.

Also bear in mind that face to face communication occurs on more than one level. Your body language, the way you dress and the way you move will also offer clues which you are transmitting and which are being picked up all the time by others.

One of the most effective forms of communication is collaboration with colleagues, ensuring that the added value of combining more than one set of effort has a cumulative effect, making it possible to disseminate good practice and information as a result.

A worrying but significant recent trend is the use of technology to substitute for what could be expected to be more human but time consuming interactions like face to face meetings or use of the telephone. At a minor level this can occur when employees in the same building prefer to communicate by email rather than going to see a colleague at their desk – and it doesn't seem to matter whether they are ten feet or ten floors away. At a more destructive level, it appears that recent mass sackings in the finance and banking sector were often carried out by email, with hundreds of individuals being dismissed in this way simultaneously. You will, no doubt, have an opinion as to where this fits on the professionalism spectrum.

CONFIDENTIALITY

Whether you are a doctor, a lawyer, a businessman or a good friend, those who share information (and opinions) with you need to know that what they say to you is safeguarded and will not be repeated. Guaranteed confidentiality is another of the cornerstone elements of professionalism.

Be known as someone to whom others can bring confidences and this automatically brings a reputation as someone who will be discrete and will not repeat information or betray a confidence. The assumption will also be that you try not to ruffle feathers and don't express potentially contentious views or indulge in gossip.

Difficulties can arise if your role as confidant comes into direct conflict with your ethical standards and your obligation to society as a whole. Making a decision on how to proceed will be a balancing act.

CONTINUING PROFESSIONAL DEVELOPMENT (CPD)

This is an investment in your future and your wellbeing so should be taken very seriously. CPD is essential and requires you to make a commitment to ongoing self-improvement.

Learning is a continuous process and does not stop once you undertake some training or achieve qualifications. Be open to ongoing growth. You should not rest on your laurels but must keep reinventing yourself by staying current. Try new things even if you don't think you need or want them. You won't know how useful they could be unless you try. Be willing to learn what you don't yet know or enhance what you know if you need more in-depth knowledge.

Read widely in order to stay abreast of current affairs, stay informed, stay up to date. Become a words and information addict!

Nor should you be afraid to ask for help in understanding what you don't yet know. It can come from many directions - professional associations, networks, those who are older and more experienced, perhaps from other disciplines, those who are younger and perhaps more in tune with newer technologies or with alternate ways of tackling issues.

In order to enhance or maintain your competence, establish a regular review process for yourself by which you update both your skills and knowledge whilst developing the various attributes we are discussing as part of the ABC for Success.

Be a thinker and indulge in some reflection and evaluation at the end of each day, each week or on completion of each task. Look at what has been achieved or the results and work out what went well and what you may need to work on to improve for next time.

Professionalism means that you are self-motivated and will maintain your networks because you are interested and not just because they are useful.
Watch who does something well and work out or ask how they do it.

 Remember – your conduct reflects well on you as an individual and on your profession as a whole

C for CHARACTER

C for CHARACTER

Each person's character is unique and is made up of a combination of personal qualities which makes us different from everyone around us. These qualities are inherent or acquired over a long period of time and define our essence, our core nature.

These qualities, the third part of the ABC for Success, contribute to the esteem in which we are held and are a major part of our reputation and respectability.

These personal qualities are our guarantee of moral quality as we interact with the world and its sometimes difficult demands.

 'You can easily judge the character of a man by how he treats those who can do nothing for him'
- *James D Miles*

To be well thought of and considered honourable by our peers and to maintain their approval means that the character we present must contain certain key features or traits.

INTEGRITY

There are often moments when we all have to admit that we are under pressure to do or be something we don't want to. As a professional you can withstand this pressure because you have made a decision to be true to yourself. You cannot be pushed, bribed or induced off course or made to do what you don't want to do because it is not in your nature. Professionals must be true to themselves because they have a set of principles by which they live and which guides their conscience in all things.

Your personal integrity means that you are above suspicion or reproach and there will never be a hint of any wrong doing or scandal attached to your name or your dealings with other people.

Professionals maintain high standards and take pride in their work. They are never afraid to set these high standards or create new ones.

 'Integrity is doing what's right even when nobody is looking'

That integrity will extend to being advocates for what they believe in and encouraging others to benefit from those beliefs.

HONESTY

Professionals are always honest and fair in what they think, say and do. At the heart of every intention is honesty about what is meant. Honesty will always be accompanied by sincerity. In most cases, personal interests are secondary to those of the individuals who are relying on you for whatever reason.

Because you are honest you are also straightforward in your approach and your dealings with people. As a consequence, people will know where they stand with you, nor are you devious and there are no hidden agendas. What you see is definitely what you get! People therefore don't need to worry that you are saying one thing but mean something quite different. You are forthright and will tell it like it is. You are also unlikely to fudge an issue so that people are clear about where you stand on any subject.

There should not be any chinks in the armour, however small, because it would not sit easily with your honest approach. You would never steal or misappropriate funds or 'work' the expense account. Think twice before taking those paperclips from the office because you know you need them at home. Acquiring stationery is not an acceptable way to boost your salary, well illustrated by a recent cautionary tale - the documented case of the executive who lost his job because he was caught on CCTV removing items from the stock room, putting them into his briefcase then leaving for home.

Professionals know that it is critically important to be honest with themselves as well as others and that their success depends on that honesty, even extending to knowing their own limits.

 Always be up front and admit if you are not able to do something. Ask for help or extra time to work out how to do it. Far better than failing and ruining your reputation.

You would like to believe that all those with whom you have dealings will be equally honest in return but this can sometimes lead to disappointments which you must rise above and move on.

LOYALTY

As professionals, your relationships with those around you are an important part of how you function on a daily basis.

These relationships include your friends and family, colleagues, clients or customers, those with whom you have activities in common - sports teams, faith groups, hobbies and activities, even fellow members of your professions.

Each individual within these different groups knows that you are dependable and can always, therefore, be relied on for support.

This loyalty is not dependent in any way on the provision of favours. You will help if asked, provide back up, tangible assistance or moral support without hesitation.

 'The best things in life are never rationed. Friendship, loyalty, love, do not require coupons'
- *George T Hewitt*

DO THE RIGHT THING

We all have expectations that people in positions of authority or power will always do the right thing. They will recognise it and act on it. However, we also all know that there have been more than a few recent public examples of the opposite behaviour and this is very disappointing.

It creates issues with establishing just who our role models ought to be. Sportsmen, celebrities and politicians have all been shown to have feet of clay. Doing the right thing, therefore, should be a guiding principle for all professionals as individuals.

It can be difficult to maintain this stance if others pressure you to do something with which you are not too comfortable. They may point out that it could be less difficult if you did not stand your ground but just knowing it is wrong will prevent you from being involved or going any further.

This can occasionally lead to circumstances where you may need to assess whether doing the right thing will cause a conflict of interest or may end up being good for one party and bad for another. All the relevant facts will need to be weighed in the balance to make a decision on the right thing to do.

These moral dilemmas are difficult for a variety of reasons and doing the right thing may have direct or indirect consequences for you personally. For instance, you may have been looking for a role and are offered an internship with an organisation which, when you do some research on them, has a questionable investment record. What will you do? What will you say?

On the other hand, the so-called "whistleblower" legislation has been designed to protect individuals who may wish to divulge information about a particular employer which is in the public interest.

Although doing the right thing is usually something which is about individual choices, a person with a fully functioning moral compass can be relied on to point everyone in the right direction, acting as the group or team's conscience.

 'Right is right, even if everyone is against it; and wrong is wrong, even if everyone is for it'
- *William Penn*

TRUTHFUL

On the whole, we are all aware that not telling the truth is unacceptable behaviour. Attempting to justify a lie by describing it as 'bending the truth' does not make it any more acceptable.

Consequently, professionals know that the truth is an absolute and this makes them reliable and dependable.

They won't lie or blame someone else to get out of difficulties and will always keep their word.

They also know that massaging the truth doesn't help anyone either. Instead of bending the truth to make a friend feel better they are more likely to just tell the truth and help the other person to face whatever the problem is that they are working their way through.

 'If you tell the truth you don't have to remember anything'

- Mark Twain

RESPONSIBILITY

Professionals accept that they are responsible for what they do and say and accept the repercussions from either. They know that someone must be accountable and, consequently, take pride in what they do in both their work and private lives.

They also accept the responsibilities inherent in a particular role and do not try to avoid them. They can be relied on to carry out a task or keep their word and accept that they are accountable for results.

They also know that they are responsible for the quality, progress and completion of any task allocated to them, whether as work projects or as social activities. They know that, if they are responsible for the work, then they are also responsible for those involved in the work, for their attitudes and the climate in which the work is carried out. In some cases, they may also be responsible for the welfare of those they work with.

They understand that errors or mistakes can happen and will accept responsibility for any which are caused by things they have done or omitted to do, taking ownership of the issue or problem caused and not making excuses. If they are responsible for a task or project which fails then they will own up to the failure, while at the same time ensuring that they learn appropriate lessons from what has gone wrong.

They know that the concepts of corporate and social responsibility are essential in safeguarding all our futures and are likely to attempt to introduce such ideas into their workplace or social group.

 Accept your responsibilities at all times
Show that you will be there – no matter what

There may be occasions when, although not responsible or accountable for a particular piece of work, they have perhaps been informed or consulted about it. Under those circumstances they understand that the responsibility will lie elsewhere but it is still worth understanding how the results affect everyone involved.

MAKE IT WORK FOR YOU

MAKE IT WORK FOR YOU

The world is constantly reinventing itself, offering huge opportunities, so this is a great time for all of us to shine. How can we make this happen?

- We know that what we do affects others
- We have an understanding of how that happens
- We have made some decisions about our future
- All our attributes are in place.

How do we ensure that others see that we have chosen the route to professionalism? Here are the decisions to make:

- Decide to choose excellence in everything you do
- Decide to be professional in all things and live it

Accept and understand that:

- **Professionalism is who you are and what you do**

- This is not a simple concept but it is fundamental

- **You are you but you can be more**

- Examples of professionalism are all around you look for them and learn from them

- **You must be as good as you say you are**

 'You must be the change you wish to see in the world'
   - *Mahatma Gandhi*

EMPATHY

The magic ingredient in the 'recipe' for professionalism is empathy – the ability to see and experience the world, and especially our behaviour, through the eyes of others.

This is a wonderful tool, offering the ability to understand the effect we have on those around us.

Consider how you make people feel in their dealings with you. What evidence do you have of the effect you are having? You can listen to what they say, you can try and read their body language, you can try and find hidden meanings in their written communications. You can probably also find some clues if they only deal with you once and never come back again!

Try to see it from their point of view. What must it be like to be on the receiving end? Would you enjoy being treated the way you have treated them? Have you provided an exemplary service by anyone's standard or just according to your own ideas and was it effective?

Have you met their expectations in what you have provided, whether it is advice and counselling for a friend or delivering a project at work? How effective has your communication with them been and have you understood them clearly in return?

 Although we can't see what others see, we can see the results of our interactions with them

Before each and every interaction, try to envisage how it might feel to be to be on the receiving end.

As a result of your ability to understand the world from another perspective, you will understand the need for compassion in your dealings with some of the people you meet. An understanding that their experience of life is intrinsically different or difficult triggers a compassionate response which may change some of your attitudes for ever. There will still be occasions, however, when you must acknowledge your compassionate or sympathetic response, let the individual see that you care but you may also need to be clear that you still have expectations that they will do their job or complete the task at hand.

SELF BELIEF

Belief in yourself and your abilities is not to be confused with arrogance. Nor is it about adopting and using an image or set of actions, much like putting on a set of clothes, which might make it appear that you could be a member of a particular profession. You do not need to do and be the same as everyone else.

Total self belief is internal and is anchored in being self confident, self aware, self controlled, self disciplined and exercising self respect, self management and self restraint.

Over time these also contribute to understanding:

- your passion for what you are doing
- your engagement with the task in hand
- the encouragement to do the best you can
- an appreciation for what you are achieving
- that small achievements are worth noting, not just bigger ones
- public recognition of your achievements
- respect earned for your achievements
- the importance of thanking and being thanked for what you contribute

On the down side, anybody's confidence can be shaken by making a mistake, whether it is large or small. It is an uncomfortable fact of life that errors and mistakes happen, however hard we try to avoid them. A professional will always admit the mistake, to himself and to others, but will then find a way to learn from the error and ensure that it is not repeated. A bit like alchemy, it is usually possible to create something good from the bad.

Professionalism also means understanding that the balance and interface between work and the rest of our lives is critically important for our health and well being. This applies to ourselves and to those around us and to those for whom we bear some responsibility. Holidays, downtime, turning the machines off, taking a walk, are all strategies to recharge the batteries and regain our perspective.

Take an occasional moment for cloud gazing and allowing yourself to enjoy the moment, whether it is appreciating some fine food, or a child's laugh or beautiful scenery. Find the time to refresh the spirit. It keeps us all positive.

QUALITY

Quality and professionalism are two sides of the same coin and are totally linked. Professionalism means dedication, focus and total commitment to the quality of the result of each task or job undertaken.

You know that you are responsible for the quality of the work entrusted to you, whether undertaking it personally or asking someone else to do it on your behalf.

You give priority to your clients or customers and inspire confidence and trust that the task will be fulfilled, clearly setting out the expectations around costs, benefits and completion.

You will utilise state of the art expertise to the highest possible standards and will check and recheck the quality and accuracy of the finished product. Paying total attention to the various levels of detail means that you don't miss things by being distracted or any lack of concentration.

The quality of your results makes you stand out from the crowd. Professionals bring added value. A potter living by himself in a cottage in the wilds of Scotland may not see a living soul from one year to the next but his craft is still exceptional and is of benefit to others.

 If someone tells you how much they appreciate the work you have done for them, ask them to provide you with a testimonial or reference document for your portfolio

Your processes and procedures will always be transparent and, consequently, you have no fear of scrutiny from any source.

ANYONE AT ANY LEVEL

Professionalism and excellence can and should exist at any level. Having power or being in a position of authority is not necessary to be effective. Anyone can initiate or be an agent for change for themselves or within their organisation at any level and in any role.

 You can lead at any level – it's not necessary to be in a position of authority

Powerlessness is merely a state of mind – shun it!

Make suggestions, make improvements, be the best you can. The benefits will filter out in all directions. We all have opportunities to make our own contribution – choose to make things better.

When your professionalism is recognised you earn the trust and respect of those around you. In turn, this will enhance your ability to influence those around you because of their willingness to listen. Most importantly, recognition will enhance your own self-respect.

 Amateurs do something till they get it right
Professionals do it till they can't get it wrong

MANAGE IMPRESSIONS

As a professional you will:

- Make people remember you
- Make people want to be with you
- Make people want to work with you

We have already said that first impressions count. Physical presence makes a huge contribution to the assumptions and decisions people make when they meet each other so make an effort to be 'well turned out', whatever your style.

If you only have a few seconds to make that first impression (and research indicates that it is as little as 7 seconds) then you need to put some effort into it.

- ✓ Dress professionally and appropriately
    - ensuring your clothes and shoes are clean and fresh
- ✓ People notice hands straight after they notice faces
    – keep them clean, nails trimmed and jewellery subtle
- ✓ Make eye contact
- ✓ Cultivate a firm handshake
- ✓ Be animated and articulate
- ✓ Radiate energy
- ✓ Engage with the person you are talking to
    - don't look around the room as if looking for someone more interesting to talk to
- ✗ Don't chew gum

Try to avoid the mobile phone minefield:

- ✓ Turn it off or to silent mode during meetings
- ✗ Don't check messages or read texts or emails during meetings
- ✗ Don't take another call during the call you are already on
- ✗ Don't sit at the back of a seminar or conference checking your phone messages
- ✗ Don't take calls in the middle of a face-to-face conversation
- ✗ Don't check to see who has left a message or whose call you have missed during a conversation – it can wait
- ✓ **No-one is more important than the person you are talking to at that moment**

This is your face-to-face or one-to-one personality.

You also need to consider your one-to-many personality, which is usually about electronic and online forms of communication. Your electronic image has just as much to say about you but there is a huge risk here as you are not present in person to either correct a bad impression or defend yourself.

Ensure that all your online profiles are consistent. Use the same biography and photograph for your various networks so that you become recognisable. Check that any recorded messages are polite – try to avoid playful or character messages as they can be very off-putting. Try dialling your own numbers to hear your electronic voice.

Digital etiquette is increasingly important. Make sure that people receive what you think you are sending and intend to communicate. Messages should be very clear to avoid confusion and remember that humour (and sarcasm) can get lost in the ether if you don't know the recipient very well.

If there is the potential for misunderstandings or difficulties then a telephone call will achieve a better result than email or text messaging in most cases.

Also remember that what you do online stays out there – be sure that you won't regret it in five years' time. Think twice about posting embarrassing or compromising pictures or making offensive or ill-judged comments. You cannot appear professional if you are using abusive or profane language online.

All of these things matter and, without stating the obvious too bluntly, we are always engaged in marketing ourselves in one way or another. So look for opportunities for promotion but keep asking yourself 'What will people remember about me?'

So invest a lot of effort in beginnings and endings – the way you enter a room, start a conversation, begin a relationship as well as your exit strategy – saying goodbye, thanking a host, promising to stay in touch, handing over a business card. Then remember to follow up in the way you have promised you will!

MANAGE RELATIONSHIPS

Unsurprisingly, manners do matter. Doing the polite or thoughtful thing will always be effective in building and maintaining relationships.

Remember to say please and thank you, especially to colleagues or staff for a job well done or for a service performed. Remember to acknowledge friends and staff birthdays. Acknowledge the contribution of others publicly. Acknowledge a job well done publicly.

The small gestures matter in our busy lives. Return phone calls and emails promptly even just to say I can't give you a full reply immediately but will get back to you within a day or so.

If things do get difficult, it is usually possible to salvage a situation. Make that call NOW, don't let it fester. It will be worse the longer you leave it so be strong and deal with it.

Use the power of 'good conversation' and make space in your day to get to know the people around you. Not just the facts but the emotions too. Take time out and spend some time with people, not just achieving your agenda items.

Asking people to participate or for their opinion can enhance results. If you understand what they would like to contribute then it becomes easier to work together.

 Be happy. There is nothing more contagious than a happy person

People like to work with people they like. If it's good for business, then that's a bonus.

A professional will be able to fit in and behave appropriately wherever they go, using all their senses to work out how to adjust to different settings and work cultures.

BE EFFECTIVE

Strong time management skills are a major element in ensuring that you achieve your scheduled commitments. There are several essential steps to make your days and weeks work for you, no matter where you are and no matter what you are trying to fit in.

- Start by building in some thinking time. It is tempting to just 'dive in' but time for reflection will be time well spent
- Construct your to do list, planning your time and giving it structure
- If you are still overloaded and are having trouble achieving what you think you should, try filling out a time sheet for a couple of days, see how much time you spend on each item, email, phone calls, even food breaks. You may need to discipline yourself or compress the time allowance a little
- Put a little contingency time in your schedule – you just never know what is coming round the corner
- Take a break – if you realise that you are getting distracted or you have read the same sentence three times then it is time to stand up and do something else, take a walk, chat to a friend, anything which will recharge your batteries.
- Make sure you get enough sleep and ensure you drink plenty of water or other fluids. You won't do your best work if you are too tired or dehydrated.

Another way to ensure that you make best use of your time is to be as organised as possible. There is nothing more frustrating than looking for something which just doesn't want to be found. Try to use the rule about handling things once only – whether it is a letter or an email, deal with it immediately. Don't put it off or you will double or treble the time spent on it or perhaps not get round to it at all.

Not everyone works best at a tidy desk but do consider what sort of impression you are making if there are piles of documents, books, mail or magazines piled up on your desk and spilling over onto the floor. Studies indicate that giving yourself some clear working space tends to unclutter the mind as well as the desktop! Is your desk covered in soft toys or are they falling off the dividers onto other people's desks? Time for a clearout. Family photographs are always acceptable but keep the content sensible and the numbers down.

Know what is expected of you, do what is needed and then do more – can you improve it, can you deliver to a higher standard? Do it better than anyone is expecting.

COMPETENCE AND EXPERTISE

Your reputation depends on ensuring that you can demonstrate your competence and are able to provide evidence of your expertise.

Add to this a willingness to continue learning from those around them and professionals remain self-sufficient and adaptable. They realise that skills gained in the workplace can be used elsewhere and that it is also possible to bring external skills into the workplace where relevant. If, for instance, your current role does not offer you much line management experience, you may be responsible for supervising a team at your local sports club. Any such experience can be relevant.

Professionals will also take the time to be of assistance to others, sharing expertise and looking for opportunities to encourage those with fewer skills or less knowledge. This may involve formal mentoring schemes or just ad hoc assistance to a friend or colleague.

Professionals seldom look for shortcuts as they are determined to do the best job possible – they will expect to earn their salary and the respect of those around them.

They are also pragmatic and realistic and know that life is not always straightforward. Being prepared for other eventualities is second nature – 'Plan B' is usually sitting somewhere in the background ready for activation! You will occasionally come across those for whom having 'Plan C' ready to go is very much a necessity.

Professionals are usually creative problem solvers who understand that there is normally more than one way to tackle something. Nor do they dig their heels in to ensure they get their own way. Their approach is usually logical and consistent and, although they are quite happy to argue their point they are equally happy to concede to a well structured argument from another viewpoint.

Above all, professionalism is not just about gaining certificates and qualifications. Although these may be an integral and necessary part of their continuing education and progression, they understand that an open enquiring mind brings its own benefits. They will understand how essential it is to continually enhance their knowledge, skills and competence in their chosen field.

CONTINUAL IMPROVEMENT

Invest in yourself. Only you are in a position to know when you need to extend your understanding or capabilities in some way. If you encounter something at which you are not yet proficient then you will need to find out how to fill that gap, either by finding the appropriate resources or seeking the detail or assistance required.

This is CPD or continuing professional development. It is important to start as early as possible to get into the good habits that adherence to CPD can bring. It should start at school, through your leisure pursuits, clubs, areas of interest and continue into the world of work.

A key element is to value your experience as it is gathered over time and value the judgement that comes with those years of experience.

Treat failures or mistakes as a way to learn. They only remain a problem area if you fail to learn anything from them.

If you see someone whose demeanour yells 'professionalism' from every pore, try to convince them to become your mentor. Ask for their help, ask them to show you, guide you, give you the benefit of their experience – it cannot be considered a short-cut as you will have to do it for yourself but it will give you the confidence to know that you are going in the right direction.

This process of continuing improvement is appropriate for everything you do. Take every opportunity you can find, read widely, use your networks whenever possible, attend seminars and conferences, stretch yourself – you never know what may be possible until you try.

GUARANTEED RESULTS

- True professionalism will get you noticed – this is good for you, good for your career progression and good for other life opportunities

- It will give you immense satisfaction – not just as an individual but also in the benefits you bring to others

- You can be extraordinary every day

- You can take pride in knowing that each and every task or job you tackle will be done well

- You will know that you did what you could to help

- You will know that you participated and made a difference

- You will know that you stood up to be counted when it mattered and weren't found wanting

The road to professionalism and excellence is a long journey, honed and improved over time and with experience. Give yourself the opportunity to experience it first hand.

'It is not the mountain we conquer but ourselves'
- *Sir Edmund Hillary*

THE GOLDEN RULES

PROFESSIONALISM MEANS:

- ✓ always striving for excellence

- ✓ being trustworthy

- ✓ being accountable and taking responsibility for your actions

- ✓ being courteous and reliable

- ✓ being honest, open and transparent

- ✓ being competent and continually learning

- ✓ always acting ethically

- ✓ always acting honourably and with integrity

- ✓ always treating others with respect

- ✓ always respecting confidentiality

- ✓ setting a good example

THE WISDOM OF OTHERS

Over the course of our history, many others have understood the concept of professionalism and expressed it in memorable and useful ways. If any of these quotes strike a chord with you or you think they might be a useful reminder then have one on your desk at work or somewhere at home and glance at them from time to time to help you when things get difficult. The Churchill quote is my personal favourite and I think I look at it most days! Feel free to add your own favourites.

'Professionalism is knowing how to do it, when to do it and actually doing it'
- *Frank Tyger*

'Nobody can prevent you from choosing to be exceptional'
- *Mark Sanborn, The Fred Factor*

'Becoming a star may not be your destiny, but being the best you can be is a goal that you can set for yourself'
- *Brian Lindsay*

'Never, never, never give up'
- *Winston Churchill*

'Act as if what you do makes a difference. It does'
- *William James'*

'Instead of making yourself a slave to the concept of a career ladder, reinvent yourself on a semi-regular basis'
- *Tom Peters*

'And as we let our own light shine, we unconsciously give others permission to do the same'
- *Nelson Mandela*

'No-one can make you feel inferior without your consent'
- *Eleanor Roosevelt*

'When you CARE, you MAKE the time'
- *Tom Peters*

'Your future depends on many things, but mostly on you'
- *Frank Tyger*

ABOUT THE AUTHOR

Susie Kay has worked in professional associations and membership organisations for many years, advising individuals and their employers on the wider aspects of professionalism and professional development. Her experience in the strategic management of these organisations has meant working with the widest range of organisational structures, cultures and stakeholder groups, including the academic community and government departments.

She was appointed Director of Professionalism for the British Computer Society in 2008 and was previously Head of Professional Development for the Association for Project Management. She has worked internationally with strategy groups addressing the issues around professionalism both for the European Union and as a member of the Certification Board of the International Project Management Association.

She is a frequent seminar and conference speaker. Her blog (www.theprofessionalismblog.com) has many regular followers and her articles on professionalism and associated subjects are published widely.

She is passionate about enhancing professionalism for all of us and this led to her founding The Professionalism Group (www.theprofessionalismgroup.co.uk) which is now working to promote understanding of the benefits of professionalism for all sectors of the economy.

FURTHER HELP

If you would like any extra information about the ideas in this book or information on how to arrange individual sessions or group seminars, please contact Susie Kay:

susiekay@theprofessionalismgroup.co.uk
www.professionalismbooks.com

It is also possible to arrange consultation sessions for your organisation and keynote talks or workshops for your conference. Please visit our website at:

www.theprofessionalismgroup.co.uk

Further titles are due out soon so do keep an eye on the website!

AND FINALLY...

Watch your thoughts; they become words.

Watch your words; they become actions.

Watch your actions; they become habits.

Watch your habits; they become character.

Watch your character; it becomes your destiny.